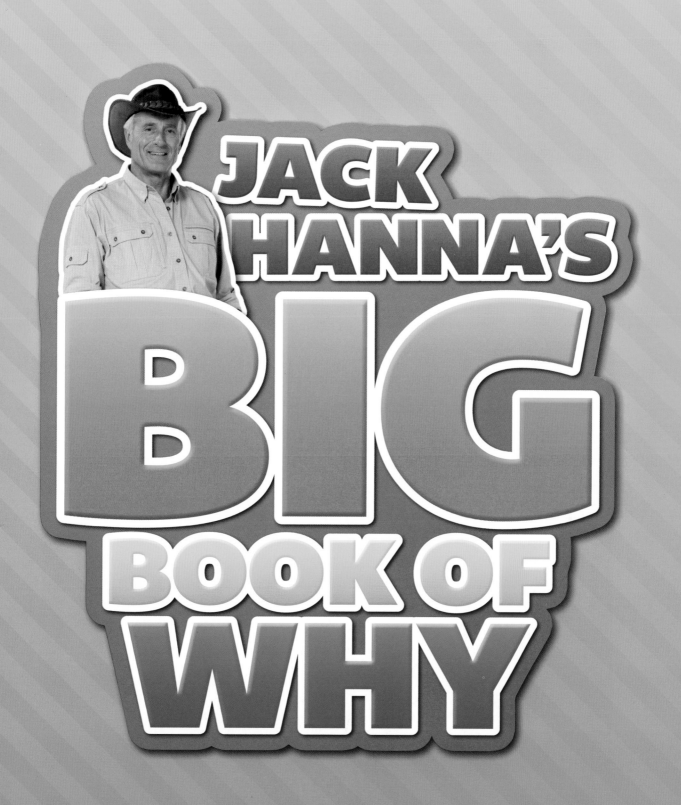

JACK HANNA'S BIG BOOK OF WHY

Hi, I'm Jack Hanna! It's my job to know a lot about animals, but even I have questions.

I started working with animals when I was 11, and I've loved them ever since. Today I'm the Director Emeritus of the Columbus Zoo and Aquarium and the host of two TV shows about animals: *Into the Wild* and *Wild Countdown*. Animals are fascinating, and every critter—from the aardvark to the zebra—makes me want to learn more. Why do elephants have such big ears? Why don't fish sink? Why do kangaroos need pouches? The answers are as weird, wacky and wonderful as the animals themselves. And I can't wait to share them with you!

TABLE OF CONTENTS

Want to learn more? Check out *jackhanna.com* today!

Welcome To The Wild!

The place where an animal lives is called its "habitat," and there are many habitats all over the world. Habitats give animals food, water and shelter— but that's where the similarities end. The varying habitats range from deserts to forests to oceans, and each is unique. They experience different weather, grow different plants and have different landscapes, which is why each is home to different animals! To put it in terms we're familiar with, habitats are like neighborhoods, and each animal prefers a specific neighborhood. Most of the time, it has to do with what each habitat has to offer. For example, because polar bears are great at staying warm and catching fish, they belong in the icy Arctic and not the hot, dry desert.

"I'm Pepe, and I'm lost!"

Pepe is a baby Emperor penguin, and the habitat where he lives is filled with snow and ice and delicious fish. Keep an eye out for Pepe throughout this book in habitats where he doesn't belong!

THE RAINFOREST

FUN FACT!
Because monkeys and gorillas like to swing from trees, they call tree-filled habitats, such as tropical rainforests, home.

THE OCEAN

THE POLES

THE GRAS

From prairies to pampas to savannahs, there's just one word for grassland animals: awesome.

FUN FACT! Temperate grasslands are found in the unlikeliest places, such as Dorset, a region in south Engand.

Key Features

1. Too little rain to be considered a forest

2. Too much rain to be considered a desert

3. Located between forests and deserts

4. Flat, open land with few trees

5. Filled with grasses, flowers and shrubs

SLANDS

Is that a cow?

Grasslands cover about 25 percent of Earth's land and can be found on every continent except Antarctica. They can be temperate or tropical and have tons of different names, from prairies to pampas to savannahs. But no matter what you call them, every grassland gets too little rain to be a forest and too much rain to be a desert. In fact, most grasslands can be found somewhere between the two habitats! Different grasslands also share similar vegetation—grass, flowers and shrubs—but are home to vastly different animals. For example, North American prairies are home to bison, which can't be found in the African savannah, where lions and zebras run rampant.

MASAI GIRAFFE

Why do giraffes have horns?

When you don't have a helmet, you have to protect your head somehow, especially when knocking noggins is commonplace. So male and female giraffes have two, hair-covered horns called **ossicones**. They come in handy when sparring with opponents. But we'll stick with helmets, thanks!

"Stop showing off, Gary!"

Why do giraffes have spots?

Just like leopards, giraffes have spots to help them blend into their surroundings. That way, they can better hide from the lions and alligators that are trying to hunt them. And even though it looks like every giraffe is rocking the same look, each animal actually has its own unique spotted pattern!

SOUND IT OUT!

Ossicones
(ah-seh-cones)

The horns on top of a giraffe's head are called ossicones, and giraffes are one of only two types of animals that have them. The other? The okapi! Even though okapis have striped legs like the zebra, they're actually more closely related to giraffes.

OKAPI

FUN FACT!
Giraffes are the world's tallest animal—their babies are taller than most humans!

Why Do Giraffes Have Such Long Necks?

Imagine having to race against your classmates every time you wanted a bite to eat. It'd be a pain in the neck! That's where giraffes' height comes in handy. Instead of fighting for leaves at the bottom of the bush with the rest of the animal kingdom, they use their long necks to reach mostly untouched tree tops. This is a huge plus when food is scarce, and it makes eating during droughts and bad weather easier.

Why Do Zebras Have Stripes?

To us, a zebra's pattern stands out, but in the African savannah, their stripes help them do the opposite. The black-and-white design acts as an optical illusion that confuses predators. When a lion sees a group of zebras from a distance, they look like one massive—and much harder to attack—zebra. Scientists think stripes might also keep zebras cool.

BURCHELL'S ZEBRA

GREVY'S ZEBRA

My family and I visited with a young zebra in South Africa while filming for *Into the Wild* in 2010!

DID YOU KNOW?
Different zebra species have different types of stripes. Some are narrow, and some are wide.

Why do zebras have mohawks?

Just like you don't look identical to your cousins, zebras don't look exactly like theirs: horses. A zebra's mohawk is really a mane, but it's much shorter than its relatives'. Its length and coarse texture, along with the size of a zebra's neck, makes the striped animal's mane stick straight up, resulting in a mohawk that never needs hair gel!

Why Do Elephants Have Such Big Ears?

The better to hear with! Elephants' ears help them pick up sound from miles away—but that's not all. Their huge ears also radiate heat to keep them cool on the hot African savannah, in addition to flapping in ways that help them communicate.

DID YOU KNOW?
Female elephants have another name, but you'd never guess it. They're also called cows!

Like elephants, other animals have tusks, too. Can you guess which?

A Walruses

B Tigers

C Cows

Check your answers on page 176!

Why Do Elephants Like Peanuts?

Don't believe everything you see on TV! Elephants don't actually like peanuts. You'd never see them eating nuts in the wild, and zoos don't feed them to elephants, either.

AFRICAN ELEPHANT

FUN FACT!
All African elephants have tusks, but some Asian elephants do not!

Why do elephants have long trunks?

With about 100,000 muscles, an elephant's giant nose is one of its most valuable assets. Usually, noses are made exclusively for smelling, but elephants use theirs to do just about everything. Their noses double as trumpets, tools and arms (complete with fingers on the end)! Go ahead. Try to pick up something with your nose. We'll wait!

Why do elephants sometimes cry?

Just like a person's eye might water when it has something in it, an elephant might cry to rid its peepers of grass or dirt. But some researchers think elephants cry for another reason, too: sadness. For example, there are many reports of baby elephants crying after being separated from family. Because we can't ask an elephant why it weeps, most scientists agree we can't be entirely sure.

ASIAN ELEPHANTS

Why do elephants like to hang out in the mud?

Who doesn't love playing in the mud every now and then? Elephants sure like it! In addition to providing good clean fun, mud baths cool elephants off and protect them from the hot African sun. And they need it. Unlike most animals, elephants can get sunburnt, and they don't have special lotions to help with the pain! For elephants, caking on a muddy layer of grime is similar to slathering on a nice thick layer of sunscreen.

Why do elephants have great memories?

Elephants need great memories for child rearing. Can you imagine if your mom forgot your babysitter? How would she know whom to leave you with? Because elephants depend on one another to communally raise their young, they're excellent at remembering who's trustworthy and who's not. In fact, elephants can recognize more than 200 different individuals—be they people or elephants. That's a lot of faces!

FUN FACT!
Oxpeckers like to dine on more than ticks, flies and lice. They love to munch on ear-wax, too!

WHITE RHINOCEROS

SOUND IT OUT!

Symbiotic
(sim-bee-ah-tick)

When two creatures (whether it's you and your pet or you and your mom) both depend on one another, that's known as a symbiotic relationship. It's usually a word reserved for different species that rely on each other, such as rhinos and oxpeckers or the clownfish and the sea anemone.

Why do birds sit on rhinoceroses?

Rhinos and oxpeckers (a type of bird) enjoy a mutual **symbiotic** relationship, meaning both animals benefit from the interaction. The birds land on rhinos for a safe place to sit and an easy meal of lice, ticks and parasites. In return, rhinos earn a cleaning and an alarm system—the birds squawk to warn them of potential danger in the distance.

Why Do Rhinos Have Horns?

Rhino horns are mostly for show, not for fighting. Instead of jewelry or hair gel, these huge animals use horns to attract mates. They also use horns to dig, spar and only rhinos know what else! Even scientists aren't 100 percent sure of every way they use their horns.

AFRICAN LION

"It's good to be the king!"

DID YOU KNOW?
If lions aren't hunting, they're probably resting. These guys sleep about 20 hours per day!

Why Do Lions Have Manes?

A lion's flowing mane is like a good haircut: If you're lucky, it might help you look more attractive. Bigger manes are hotter and more physically exhausting, so only the most in-shape lions can pull them off. Because the fittest males have the fullest manes, they are the most attractive to the female lions in their habitat.

Lions are the second biggest cat in the world! What's the first?

- **A** Pumas
- **B** Tigers
- **C** Cheetahs

Check your answers on page 176!

While filming *Into the Wild* in South Africa in 2010, we were lucky to see a family of white lions. White lions are the same species as the traditional tawny-colored lions, but they have a loss of pigment (and are not albino).

FUN FACT!
Female serval cats stick together, too! Moms kick their sons out about a year and a half before they do their daughters.

Why Do Lions Live In Groups?

Lions are incredibly social. They live in groups called prides, which include a couple males and about a dozen females, along with their cubs. They work together for efficiency's sake to hunt, raise their cubs and defend their turf.

Why don't lions have "cat eyes?"

Big cats like lions and tigers are different than house cats. They have round pupils good for daytime vision that protect their eyes from taking in too much sunlight. They can also expand their pupils for night vision.

Why are there so many lionesses with just one lion?

Lion prides are full of girl power, with more than twice as many girls as boys. Unlike females, who stay with their prides until they die, males are kicked out after a few years. Jealous and **territorial**, the pride's males want to avoid competition. Unfortunately, it's harder for males to survive in the wild.

SOUND IT OUT!

Territorial (teh-rih-tore-ee-uhl)

When an animal is territorial, that means it doesn't want unwelcome guests to hang out on its turf—particularly guests that are the same species. Territorial animals, such as lions, tigers and ring-tailed lemurs, fight to keep intruders out!

AMERICAN BISON

Why do bison have that big hump on their backs?

A bison's big hump is made of lots of muscles. Just like we use our muscles to lift heavy objects and run long distances, bison use their muscles for physical activity, too. The muscles allow bison to easily move their heads in any direction. This ability is especially handy during snowy winters, when bison use their heads as snowplows, pushing bunches of snow aside and out of their way.

Why do baboons have colorful rear ends?

Baboon behinds might look like they hurt, but they're not the result of injury. Instead, they're a special evolutionary adaptation the monkeys have developed over time. Because baboons spend most of their days sitting, their tough red bottoms double as built-in seats. Sounds comfortable, right? Well, to them it is! Baboons can sit for hours at a time without getting sore behinds.

HAMADRYAS BABOON

NAKED MOLE RAT

Why do naked mole rats look so weird?

With wrinkly skin, protruding front teeth and little eyes, naked mole rats have an ugly reputation. Because they live underground, they don't need fur to stay warm. Additionally, they use their long buck teeth to tunnel through the earth and their sunken eyes to keep dirt out of their eyes. As weird as they might look, these features help the rodents live for up to 30 years—about 10 times longer than their rodent relatives!

Why Do Some Animals Have Tusks?

DID YOU KNOW?
Though they don't eat meat, warthogs are very tough and have been known to kill predators that come after them.

Tusks are huge, sturdy teeth that poke out of an animal's mouth. These valuable tools come in handy for everything from self-defense to intimidation to gathering food. Unfortunately, animal tusks can be useful to humans, too. Hunting animals for their tusks has always been common, though it is illegal.

EUROPEAN BISON

Why don't buffalo have wings?

You're probably wondering how those hot, spicy, delicious wings got their name if they didn't come from a buffalo. Really, buffalo wings are made of chicken, but the food was created in Buffalo, New York. How did the city get its name? Some people think that bison, which settlers called buffalo, used to roam the area.

DID YOU KNOW?
Buffalo roam to find water, too. Unlike some animals, these big guys need to rehydrate every day. Too bad they don't have water bottles!

Why Do Buffalo Roam?

Buffalo are grazers that eat lots of grass, shrubs and other vegetation. Because they eat so much, they have to move from place to place to find fresh lawn they haven't already mowed down with their mouths.

AMERICAN BISON

FUN FACT!
Kangaroos' big, strong tails are great for balance, which makes them great at boxing.

Why Do Kangaroos Jump?

Kangaroos' legs are like reflections—whatever one does, the other has to do, too. Kangaroos can't help it! Because they can't move one leg without moving the other, hopping is about the only option they have for getting around. Luckily, kangaroos are good at it. They can hop faster than 35 miles per hour and higher than 25 feet in the air. That's as fast as a bengal tiger and as high as a standard flagpole!

Why do kangaroos have pouches?

Because they don't have strollers! Female kangaroos sport a pouch on their belly in order to hold their children, which are called joeys. When joeys are born, they're only about the size of a grape! They leave their mothers' pouches for the first time when they're around 4 months old, popping out for short periods of time. At 10 months, joeys leave the pouch for good.

DID YOU KNOW?
Kangaroos swipe and punch at several opponents—even other kangaroos. Males even punch each other to impress female kangaroos. With their strong legs, they kick, too!

Why Are Cheetahs So Fast?

Cheetahs are the fastest land animal on the planet. They can run up to 70 miles per hour—that's more than twice as quick as the fastest human! Cheetahs depend on their speed to hunt, so their lean, muscular bodies are built for it. They have powerful legs, big hearts and hard pads on the bottoms of their feet. Their lungs hold loads of air, so they almost never run out of breath, and their long tails help them stay balanced.

DID YOU KNOW?
Whether I'm filming cheetahs in Africa or watching them zoom around the Columbus Zoo's watering hole, when cheetahs sprint, they almost look like they're flying. They stride more than 20 feet at a time. That's longer than a car!

FUN FACT!
Cheetah feet are like cleats. Their claws give them a great grip while they're running.

CHEETAH

FUN FACT!
Ostriches are the largest birds in the world. Males can weigh more than 250 pounds!

Why Do Ostriches Bury Their Heads In The Ground?

Ostriches don't bury their heads in the sand. If they did, they wouldn't be able to breathe! With large bodies and small heads, ostriches' noggins only look buried when they pick at the ground to make nests or turn their eggs. But really, it's an optical illusion!

COMMON OSTRICH

Why don't ostriches ever fly?

They couldn't, even if they wanted to. Because ostriches have huge bodies and puny wings, flying is pretty impossible. To take to the sky, they'd have to board an airplane—but they would probably have trouble buying their tickets! Instead, ostriches use their little wings for balancing while they run and for attracting mates during courtship.

Why don't prairie dogs look like regular dogs?

Prairie dogs aren't dogs at all! Instead, they're little rodents that live underground—so the reason they don't look anything like puppies is because they're a totally different species! But they do share one characteristic with dogs: They bark just like them! When prairie dogs warn their family members danger's afoot, they make a sound similar to the ones dogs make when they bark.

PRAIRIE DOG

Why do turkeys have that weird thing hanging off their beaks?

WILD TURKEY

That weird little colorful thing is called a wattle, and, for turkeys, it's both cool and manly—literally. A turkey's wattle lets off heat to help keep the bird at a comfortable temperature during warm weather. Additionally, male turkeys have bigger, brighter wattles, which they use impress other birds like them, particularly females.

Why are antelopes such fast runners?

Antelopes don't have a choice: they have to be fast! Antelope species, like the impala, are some of the quickest mammals on land. Impalas can run more than 35 miles per hour and travel for miles upon miles at about half that speed. Because coyotes and bobcats would love to eat an antelope for dinner, speed is important to their survival. Thanks to their quickness, they can easily outrun predators.

IMPALA

BALD EAGLE

FUN FACT!
You won't find any bald eagles in Asia! Bald eagles are the only eagle unique to North America.

Can you guess where you might spot a bald eagle?

A) **England**

B) **Canada**

C) **Australia**

Check your answers on page 176!

Why Aren't Bald Eagles Bald?

If you've ever seen a bald eagle, the national symbol of the United States, you know the bird's not bald. Instead, its head is covered with white feathers. The eagle's name says more about how long the bird has been around than what it looks like. The name comes from the extremely old English word for white, "balde." Although the word fell out of fashion, the name stuck!

DID YOU KNOW?
In the late 1970s bald eagles were on the brink of extinction in the continental United States. The Columbus Zoo worked to assist the U.S. Fish and Wildlife Service in growing wild populations and today bald eagles are no longer on the endangered species list.

Why Do Some Cows Have Spots?

Despite their name, horseflies bother cows, too. They swarm animals like horses and cows—sometimes they even bite! Ouch! Researchers think a cow's spots are designed to confuse horseflies and make them a less attractive target to the pests.

HOLSTEIN COW

JERSEY COWS

Why do cows have udders?

Baby cows, or calves, like milk almost as much as you—maybe even more! After a female cow becomes a mother, she starts making milk, which comes out of her udders. The main purpose of a cow's udders, along with the milk inside them, is to feed calves. Do you know what that means? Male cows, also called bulls, don't have any udders!

Why do cowboys ride horses?

For one, horses—a cowboy's preferred mode of transportation—are easier to ride than cows because of the way they run. Plus, horses are faster, smarter and easier to train than cows are. So why aren't they called "horse boys?" Because they're named after what they do, not what they ride: Cowboys are responsible for large herds of cattle.

A filly is a young female horse. Can you guess what a colt is?

A A young male horse

B An old female horse

C An adult male horse

Check your answers on page 176!

ARABIAN HORSE

Why Do Horses Sleep Standing Up?

Although sleeping on your feet wouldn't be too comfy for you, to a horse it's like sleeping on a cloud. When horses doze off, their legs lock, so they're completely relaxed. In fact, they like to sleep standing more than they do lying down. Because they have delicate bones, horses can hurt themselves if they sleep on the ground.

DID YOU KNOW?
Because horses' eyes are on the sides of their heads, they can see nearly 360 degrees at once!

THE DESERT

The hottest parts of the Earth are home to some of the coolest animals on the planet.

Phew, It's Hot!

Deserts are known for their rainfall—specifically, their lack of it! They get fewer than 10 inches of precipitation each year, so most are hot and dry. The habitat covers about one-third of Earth's land and exists on every continent, even cold ones. In fact, Antarctica is the world's biggest desert. The largest hot desert, the Sahara, is in northern Africa. At 3.6 million square miles, the Sahara is almost as big as the United States! But there are deserts in the U.S., too. The Great Basin Desert takes up nearly all of Nevada, as well as parts of Utah, California, Idaho and Oregon. Deserts are home to unique wildlife—such as camels, roadrunners and scorpions—that thrive in the harsh conditions.

FUN FACT!
Gila woodpeckers, natives of the southwest U.S., make their homes in cactuses.

Key Features

1. Less than 10 inches of rainfall per year

2. Clear skies with little cloud cover

3. Dry, barren, reddish soil or sand

4. Few trees and other vegetation

5. Freezing temperatures at night

PATOOIE!

Why Do Camels Spit?

Dogs bark, cats hiss and camels spit. Unlike people, camel spit is more than just slobber. It's a mixture of saliva and stomach juice that they propel at anyone or thing they feel is a threat. Ew! It's a pretty clear signal to keep your distance, and camels use this trick for everything from defending their food to protecting themselves.

DROMEDARY CAMELS

BACTRIAN CAMEL

Why do some camels have more humps than others?

Just like some cars have two seats and others have five, some camels have one hump and others have two. It all depends on the species, Dromedary or Bactrian. Which is which? Dromedary camels have backs shaped like a sideways letter "D," and Bactrian camels, which are endangered, have backs shaped like a sideways letter "B."

Why can camels go so long without water?

A person is supposed to drink about half a gallon of water each day. But camels drink 40 times that—20 gallons— each time they're thirsty! They store the water in their bloodstream and don't need to drink again for weeks. Because deserts are so dry, this is important to camels' survival. Without it, they'd be unbearably thirsty.

DID YOU KNOW?
Camels don't store water in their humps. That's a myth! The humps are filled with fat from a camel's last meal. That way, they can go longer without food.

Why Don't Desert Animals Get Too Hot?

Desert animals have tons of tricks to stay cool. For example, jackrabbits release heat from their oversized ears. Others hide in the shade or burrow underground to escape the high temps. Most animals spend their days resting. Then, after sundown, they become active because it's not as hot.

SOUND IT OUT!

Nocturnal
(NOCK-ter-NAL)

Nocturnal means "occurring or active at night." Many animals are nocturnal, including bats, owls and possums. If you're caught up past your bedtime, try telling your parents you're nocturnal. Good luck!

WHITE-TAILED JACKRABBIT

FUN FACT!
Jackrabbits are **nocturnal** and feed from dusk to dawn. Otherwise, they rest in the shade. You probably won't be surprised to learn a few rabbits have been named after me, including one at the Columbus Zoo!

Why do scorpions look so scary?

Much like snakes, scorpions use venom for hunting and protection, and they couldn't put up much of a fight if their sting wasn't dangerous. Then there's the claws. Scorpions use their claws, called pincers, the same way people use their hands: to grab stuff. Scorpions grab their prey with their pincers so they can't get away, and then they use their tail to sting. Watch out for these little guys!

EMPEROR SCORPION

Why do vultures eat other animals' leftovers?

GRIFFON VULTURE

One bird's trash is another birds treasure—or their food. Vultures can eat rotten animals because they have special chemicals in their stomachs that kill the bacteria, which forms when it's been out in the sun for too long. Because they're one of the only animals that can do this, vultures take advantage of the skill and let other predators worry about the hard part of getting food—catching it in the first place.

Why do meerkats live underground?

What sounds better to you: Living in the hot desert without any shelter or living in an air-conditioned fort with tons of secret passageways and escape routes? Like you probably would, meerkats prefer the cool fort! They live underground to stay safe and out of the heat. Their tunnel networks protect them from predators by keeping them concealed, and shades them from the hot rays of the sun.

MEERKAT

Why Do Spotted Hyenas Laugh?

Unlike people, hyenas don't laugh at jokes. Your best material won't even get a chuckle out of them! In fact, hyenas laugh for the opposite reason that humans do. They laugh when they're frustrated or nervous. For example, you might hear a hyena giggle if his brother is trying to steal his food. In that situation, his "hee-hee-hee" would really mean "leave me alone!" Additionally, although hyenas are well-known for their chuckle, only spotted hyenas do it. Other species don't!

DID YOU KNOW?
Hyenas are flexible! They live in deserts, grasslands, forests and other habitats.

HA HAHA HA HA HA!

Can you guess
which kind of hyena
is most common?

A The spotted hyena

B The striped hyena

C The brown hyena

Check your answers
on page 176!

FUN FACT!
Although dorcas are the smallest species of gazelle, they have the longest limbs.

DORCAS GAZELLE

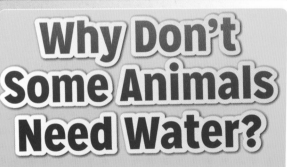

Why do turtles have shells?

For the same reason people wear bike helmets: Shells keep turtles safe. Because they're slow movers, turtles would be easy targets for dangerous predators without their suits of armor.

Why Don't Some Animals Need Water?

Nothing's more refreshing on a hot day than a cool glass of water—unless you're a Dorca gazelle, that is. Instead of wishing for water when they're thirsty, dorcas go for food. Although they'll drink water if it's available, Dorcas can get all the water they need from the leaves and flowers they eat.

Why would anyone want to live inside a cactus?

What better place to live in the hot, dry desert than inside of a cool, moist cactus? It's like having air conditioning and running water! There, Gila woodpeckers have a safe, cool place to raise their kids. They use their long beaks to break into the cactus and clear out an area to build a nest. Because few animals can do the same, there's not too much competition for the real estate. Home, sweet prickly home!

GILA WOODPECKER

Why are some animals cold-blooded? And what does that mean?

Being cold-blooded is a huge plus in the desert heat. To keep cool, cold-blooded animals (like lizards) just have to become inactive. Plus, cold-blooded animals need a lot less energy to function than warm-blooded animals. That means they need less food and water, which is hard to come by in the desert to begin with.

Why do some owls live in the ground?

Not all birds live in trees. Instead, some—such as burrowing owls—live underground. Sometimes they make their nests themselves, but most of the time they call the abandoned burrows of prairie dogs and skunks home. There, they can live safely by scaring away predators with noises that sound like the ones rattlesnakes make. Added bonus: The burrows are a lot cooler than a nest in a tree would be.

BURROWING OWL

Why Do Desert Animals Look So Skinny?

A chubby desert animal would be similar to you wearing your winter coat in the middle of summer! They'd simply be too hot. Because fat makes animals warmer, most desert inhabitants, like fennec foxes, don't have much of it. And if they do have any extra fat, they store it in one spot, like camels do in their humps.

Fennec foxes are small! Can you guess how much they weigh?

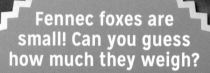

A As much as an apple

B As much as a football

C As much as a toaster

Check your answers on page 176!

FENNEC FOX

DUNG BEETLE

Why do dung beetles like playing with poop?

They aren't playing—but it's still pretty gross. Poop has everything dung beetles need, from a cool place to rest their feet to a home to lay their eggs and raise their young to a tasty treat that gives them nutrients to survive. In fact, dung beetles don't eat or drink anything else, and they love dung so much that they've been known to steal each other's piles. In the end, dung beetles' survival depends on poop. Yuck!

Why do coyotes howl at the moon?

Although it might look like coyotes are howling to no one in particular, they're really talking to their family members—and sometimes their foes. But because coyotes can't use words like people can, they use their iconic wails to communicate instead. Coyotes might howl to tell their fellow pack members to come reunite with them, or they might cry to warn members of another pack to stay off their turf.

COYOTE

Why are tarantulas' bodies so hairy?

ROSE HAIR TARANTULA

Don't let their eight eyes fool you. Spiders have terrible sight and no glasses! To make up for it, tarantulas are covered with hair, which they use as a booster for their other senses. They get a feel for the world around them thanks to the fuzz, which can taste, feel and sense moisture and vibrations. If people had skills like that, we'd never want a haircut!

CALIFORNIA KINGSNAKE

Why Are There So Many Different Kinds Of Snakes?

Just like there are different types of dogs—from Golden Retrievers to Poodles—there are lots of different snakes. Some are huge and red, while others are little and green. For example, rattlesnakes are venomous and make noise to warn others. That way, everyone knows not to bother them. It's their way of saying, "Hey! Step off, buddy!" Because snakes don't have arms or legs, they have to use other means, like venom, to protect themselves and catch food.

KING COBRA

PRAIRIE RATTLESNAKE

DID YOU KNOW?
There are about 3,000 different kinds of snakes, and none of them have eyelids!

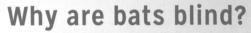

BECHSTEIN BAT

Why are bats blind?

You've probably heard the expression, "She's blind as a bat," but bats aren't really blind. Because they're nocturnal, they just don't use their eyes much. No animal can see in the pitch dark, so instead of depending on their eyesight, bats use their mouths to find their way through the darkness. The trick is called **echolocation**, and bats use it to bounce sound off nearby objects to tell where they are.

Why are bats only out at night?

When the rest of the world is turning in, most bats are just waking up. Hunting at night keeps them safe from predators, and it means less competition for food.

SOUND IT OUT!

Echolocation (eh-co-lo-cay-shun)

Echolocation is the process of using sounds to explore the world around you. Animals like bats and dolphins use echolocation to "see" a lot farther than their eyes allow. Humans use echolocation too! Modern submarines are equipped with machines that help their drivers know where to go when they're deep underwater.

DID YOU KNOW?
Since most humans sleep at night, it is hard to observe nocturnal animals. Many zoos, including the Columbus Zoo, have special places called nocturnal buildings that allow visitors to see cool animals like bats, tree kangaroos and wombats during the day!

Why Do Bats Sleep Upside Down?

Bats sleep upside down for two main reasons. The position hides them from predators, and it makes it easier for them to fly away when they need to. Plus, beds and blankets would weigh them down!

Want to sleep over?

Yeah! Let's hang out!

LESSER MOUSE-EARED BATS

GILA MONSTER

Monsters galore!
Can you guess where
Gila monsters call home?

A Arizona

B The Moon

C North Dakota

Check your answers
on page 176!

Why Don't Desert Animals Move Some Place That's Not So Hot?

How would you feel about living underwater? It might be fun at first, but your house would be all sandy and wet! Rocky land and warm weather are all desert animals, such as the Gila monster, know. They thrive in their environment, and living anywhere else would be a struggle. It's hot, but it's home.

DID YOU KNOW?
Weighing up to five pounds, Gila monsters are the largest land lizards in the United States.

THE DESERT

Top Nurse

Best Hole Digger

Head Guard

Food Finder

Why Are Meerkats So Close With Their Family Members?

Just like people, meerkat communities depend on cooperation to succeed, and these communities are made up of families. Each meerkat has a job that helps things go smoothly. Some are guards, while others are babysitters or nurses. But they all pitch in and help their communities thrive.

Fur Groomer

Lead Babysitter

GREATER ROADRUNNER

FUN FACT!
Once a roadrunner finds a mate, it stays with that bird for life.

Why Don't Roadrunners Fly?

Unlike most birds, roadrunners have short, rounded wings that can only carry them short distances. But they're so good at running—just like in the cartoon—they don't need to fly often! They sprint up to 17 miles per hour instead.

Why do skunks always smell so bad?

When was the last time you drooled over some old moldy meat? Probably never. No one wants to eat stinky food. Skunks know that, so they embrace their stench. If they feel like they're about to get eaten, they pump out a spray that sends a pretty clear message: "I don't taste good, so stay away!" After five or six stink bombs, skunks take about 10 days to replenish their scent. If you see one, don't pet it, or you might stink, too!

Peee-yew!

STRIPED SKUNK

DESERT TORTOISE

Why aren't desert animals dripping in sweat?

Sweaty animals are tough to spot—unlike humans, most animals don't sweat at all! Because water is so scarce, desert animals' bodies are programmed to save every drop. For example, some animals, like the desert tortoise, can reabsorb the water from their bladders or from the air that they breathe. Desert animals don't drink very much water in the first place, so these adaptations, which keep them hydrated, are especially handy.

Why do caracals have such hairy ears?

In the blazing desert, you'd think hair in your ears would be a hassle. But not for caracals! Scientists aren't sure what the ear hair is for, but some think the tufts are like whiskers, allowing the caracal, also known as a desert lynx, to detect things around its head. Others think the hair helps with their already great hearing. Either way, caracals look pretty cool, and their hair comes in handy.

CARACAL

Why Would An Animal Who Only Eats Plants Want To Live In The Desert?

Deserts don't have many plants, but **herbivores** still call them home. Each animal has its own trick to get enough food. Some eat very little, while others eat things fellow herbivores won't—like saltbush, which is filled with more salt than a gulp of ocean water! The viscacha—a rodent related to the chinchilla—is one of the few animals that can eat saltbush, thanks to its teeth, which strip salt from the plant's leaves. If their teeth don't do the trick, viscachas get rid of excess salt in their system by going "number 1."

DID YOU KNOW?
Viscachas aren't great at digging, so they make their homes in mountain crevices instead!

SOUND IT OUT!
Herbivore
(err-buh-vohr)

An herbivore is an animal that loves grasses and leaves and doesn't eat any kind of meat. There are lots of animals in the wild that are herbivores, including cows, rabbits, elephants, camels and deer. A human who is an herbivore is usually called a vegetarian.

Which of these animals is not an herbivore?

A Red Panda

B Mountain Lion

C Jackrabbit

Check your answers on page 176!

VISCACHA

THE FOREST

Even when seasons change, most of the amazing animals that fill this habitat stay the same.

Key Features

FUN FACT!
Rotting leaves and plants help enrich forest soil, so trees can grow strong roots.

1. No extreme temperatures

2. Filled with trees, shrubs and bushes

3. Floor covered with fertile soil

4. Four distinct seasons with different weather

5. Gets 30 to 60 inches of precipitation per year

Look at all those trees!

Chock full of greenery, most temperate, or mild, forests exist in North America, Asia and Europe. This tree-filled habitat gets about 30 to 60 inches of precipitation each year—second only to tropical rainforests—and experiences four seasons. Although each season has different weather, forests don't see the extreme temperatures other habitats do. That sure makes life easier for the animals that live here! From the badgers and deer roaming the forest floor to the squirrels and chipmunks frolicking in the trees and the birds flying above it all, forest animals are as diverse as the habitat itself!

BARRED OWL

Why Do Owls Say "Who?"

It's called a hoot. Although most people associate an owl's hoot with common curiosity, different kinds of owls make their own distinct sounds. Great horned owls say "who," while barn owls, for example, screech. The Barred owl is sometimes called an Eight Hooter because of its distinct, eight-beat cry. Owls make noise for the same reason we do: to communicate. The noises they make could be warnings, mating calls or greetings.

FUN FACT!
Owls can't see things close to their eyes clearly. They're farsighted!

BURROWING OWL

Why can owls turn their heads so far around?

Owls don't have eyes in the back of their heads, but they can put them there! Owls can rotate their necks up to 270 degrees in each direction. That's almost a full circle! Owls are so flexible because their heads are only connected by one socket, whereas our heads are connected by two.

Why do owls sleep during the day?

Not all owls are nocturnal, but most species, like Tawny owls, are. With great hearing and large pupils that help them gather lots of light, owls are best suited for hunting at night. Luckily, most of their favorite meals—squirrels, rabbits and mice—keep the same schedule, so finding food is easy. Owls hunt under the cover of darkness with the help of their stealthy, silent feathers.

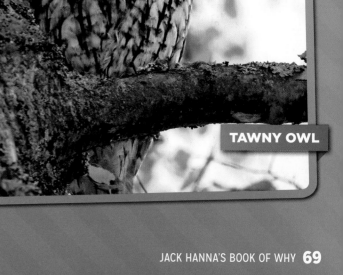

TAWNY OWL

NORTH AMERICAN RACCOON

"Give me all your garbage, and no one gets hurt!"

Why Do Raccoons Have Masks?

People wear masks on Halloween, but raccoons wear them every day! Although their faces have earned them the nickname "the masked bandits," raccoons' dark markings are designed to help camouflage themselves from predators. It's just coincidence that the masks match raccoons' sneaky personalities. They've been known to wreak havoc in neighborhoods by eating seeds from bird feeders and rummaging through trash cans with their agile paws.

Can you guess what you call a group of raccoons?

A A nursery

B A party

C A cocoon

Check your answers on page 176!

DID YOU KNOW?
Raccoons aren't picky, and their diets depend on their habitats. In cities, they'll eat trash!

AMERICAN MARTEN

Why do some animals live in trees?

Hiding in a tree might not be the best way to win a game of hide and seek, but it's the perfect place for many animals, like martens, to hide from predators that live on the forest floor. Because wolves, one of the animals that hunts the species, can't climb trees, martens' homes are safe. Living in trees has other perks, too. For example, animals who call hollow trees home have a great place to store their stuff!

Why do rats have such long tails?

A rat would have no problem on a balance beam—that's what their tails are for. Not gymnastics, but balance! Thanks to their tails, rats can navigate narrow cliff ledges and little tree limbs all around the forest. Rats' tails also help keep them cool. When they're too warm, heat flows to their tails and then out of their bodies. No AC necessary, which is good—because the forest doesn't have any!

BROWN RAT

Why do chipmunks have chubby cheeks?

No one looks cute with a mouth stuffed full of food—except for a chipmunk! Their iconic, chubby cheeks are essentially travel bags filled with snacks. They fill their cheeks with insects, nuts, berries, seeds, fruit and grain to take home and save for later. When chipmunks aren't carrying food in their cheeks, they look a little different: they're smaller. The more food they have in there, the bigger their cheeks!

EASTERN CHIPMUNK

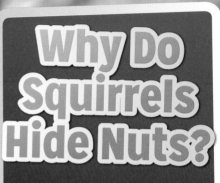

Why Do Squirrels Hide Nuts?

There aren't grocery stores in the forest, so squirrels have to plan their meals months in advance. They store food in the fall, so they won't run out of nuts to eat during winter when trees are bare and pickings are slim.

Why can some squirrels fly?

Flying is for the birds, but some squirrels are pretty good at it, too. Technically, flying squirrels like this one glide. They don't have wings to flap like birds or bats, but they do have stretchy pieces of skin between their arms and legs that they use to sail through treetops and easily avoid grounded predators.

DID YOU KNOW?
Squirrels are related to lots of other animals, including prairie dogs, marmots and chipmunks.

Why Do Rabbits Have Long Ears?

Bunnies can pick up noise from up to 32 football fields away. Plus, they can rotate their ears to make sounds even clearer. But those huge ears do way more than listen! They're packed with blood vessels that give off heat to keep bunnies cool. Because rabbits can't sweat or pant, their ear trick is incredibly important!

FUN FACT!
Rabbits can rotate their ears up to 270 degrees to better detect sounds.

EUROPEAN RABBIT

Why do rabbits eat carrots?

Carrots are sweet treats rabbits usually don't eat. That'd be like a person eating chocolate for every meal! In the wild, rabbits typically stick to flowers, hay, grass and other greens.

EASTERN COTTONTAIL RABBIT

Why do rabbits like to hop?

A hopping bunny might look like a kid who's eaten too much sugar, but for rabbits, hopping is efficient and natural. Cottontail rabbits' strong legs can bounce them up to 18 miles per hour, which comes in handy when they need to get somewhere in a flash—like when they're running away from animals who think they look like a tasty treat.

Why Do Birds Sing In The Morning?

For birds, singing is a part of life. It's how they find mates and claim territories. But the animals are especially musical in the early morning—you've probably even woken up to their melodic chirping! Scientists have lots of ideas about why birds sing more in the morning. One theory is that birds use the dim light of dawn for social interaction instead of hunting. Another suggests birds sing first thing in the morning to let others know they're strong, healthy survivors of the night. Finally, some scientists think the relative quiet in the morning makes communication easier.

Not every bird can sing. Can you guess which type can't?

A **Cardinals**

B **Finches**

C **Ostriches**

Check your answers on page 176!

BRAMBLING FINCH

"You are the wind beneath my wiiiiings!"

DID YOU KNOW?
Bramblings' calls are sharp, harsh and hard to describe. Instead of tweeting, they chirp.

DOWNY WOODPECKER

CANADA GEESE

FUN FACT!
Downy woodpeckers are the most common kind in North America.

Why do birds fly in a v-shape formation?

It's like a very efficient game of follow the leader. The birds move in sync to catch the wind of the bird in front of them, which helps them save energy during flight.

Why Do Woodpeckers Peck?

Woodpeckers use their strong beaks to break into trees, where they can find food and create nests. Pecking has other purposes, too. When you hear woodpeckers rhythmically drumming, they're probably trying to establish territory or attract mates.

Why don't birds have ears like we do?

Birds do have ears—they just don't look like ours. If you were to move back the feathers on the side of a bird's head, you'd see a canal just like the ones inside people's ears. Where we have external ears to help guide sound into our heads, birds have feathers that cover their ear canals, which cut down on wind noise when they fly. If they had external ears, flying would be too noisy.

CARMINE BEE-EATERS

CARDINALS

Why do birds build nests?

Birds can't sit with their eggs all the time, but they still want their babies to be safe, so they make nests. Nests are hard-to-reach hideouts that house eggs and newly hatched chicks. The home of twigs and sticks gives bird babies a safe place to hide from predators while their mothers search for food. When birds don't have children to tend to, they rarely build nests. Instead, they spend their time flying from tree to tree and searching for food for themselves.

Why do birds like eating worms so much?

Actually, they don't. Worms are by no means a bird's favorite food. To them, worms are kind of like hot dogs. They're not always a bird's first choice, but they're quick and easy to find and catch—plus they're packed with protein. Most of the tasty insects birds love to eat are speedy and difficult to nab, so oftentimes they have to settle for worms from the forest floor or go hungry.

ROBIN

VIRGINIA OPOSSUM

FUN FACT!
Baby possums are tiny! In fact, when a possum is born, it can be as small as a honeybee.

"Look ma, no hands!"

Why Do Possums Hang Upside Down?

Although you might see a possum dangle by its tail in cartoons, you probably won't see one in real life—unless it's a youngster. Young possums sometimes hang by their tails, but not for long periods of time. It's tough! Possums are pretty heavy, and comparatively, the muscles in their tails are weak.

DID YOU KNOW? Although they are often referred to as "possums," the animal's name is technically "opossum."

FUN FACT!
Goats don't have front teeth in their upper jaws, and kids lose teeth like us!

Why Do Goats Scream Like Humans?

It doesn't take much to make a goat yell. Kid goats scream when they want their mother, and other goats scream when they're hungry. But not all goats sound like humans. Each has a distinct voice, just like people—some just happen to sound human.

My wife Suzi and I love seeing mountain goats on our hikes in Northwest Montana!

Why can mountain goats climb so well?

With the ability to climb higher than the Empire State Building in less than 20 minutes (without stairs!), mountain goats are built for climbing. Their hooves, which are made of two sturdy rubber-like toes, give them great grip, and their muscular bodies help them easily navigate rocky terrain. In fact, they're better at climbing cliffs than they are at running over flat land.

GRIZZLY BEAR

Why Do Bears Growl?

Bears don't usually growl, but you should watch out when they do! When they feel scared or stressed, bears roar in an attempt to fix things. It's like they're saying, "Leave me alone, please!" Grizzly bears, or brown bears, growl more often than black bears.

ASIATIC BLACK BEAR

FUN FACT!
Despite their size, grizzly bears have been clocked running at 30 mph!

Why do bears stand on their hind legs?

Just because a bear's standing on his back legs doesn't mean he's going to attack. He's trying to get a better grasp on his surroundings, just like a person at the top of a watchtower. From his hind legs, a bear will assess the situation and go from there.

THE FOREST

Why Do Porcupines Have Quills?

Porcupine quills—which can be up 1 foot long—tell predators that porcupines are no easy meal. An animal would have to fight through the pain to take a bite. Approach at your own risk!

Why do deer have antlers?

Antlers probably started off as weapons for deer to protect themselves, but they're hardly used that way anymore. Female deer don't even have them! Nowadays, they're a status symbol, kind of like a king's crown. Bigger antlers intimidate other deer and attract female mates.

DID YOU KNOW?
You'll find porcupines all over the world, from Asia to Europe, Africa to North and South America.

Why do birds lay eggs instead of giving birth?

It's pretty hard to run when you're carrying something heavy, but it's even harder to fly! Just ask a bird. Like airplanes, birds can't leave the ground if they've got too much cargo on board. That would be a problem for most birds, whose lifestyles depend on their ability to soar. On the ground, they'd struggle to eat, travel and protect the babies inside them, so instead, all 900 species of birds lay eggs.

AMERICAN PEKIN DUCK

Why do some animals hibernate?

HEDGEHOG

Winter can be hard to bear even when you have a big-puffy coat—and animals don't! To stay warm during the coldest part of the year, some animals fall into a deep sleep that helps them save energy and stay warm. While hibernating, animals reduce their body temperatures and remain inactive. They can stay this way for days, weeks or even months. Imagine how hungry they must be when they wake up!

Why do possums sometimes play dead?

It's not an act, and possums can't help it. When a possum feels stressed—like when its being chased or attacked—he goes into shock and turns limp, just like a person who has fainted. As annoying as the reaction might seem, it comes in handy because the possum's predators think the rodent is dead, which makes him unappealing. Instead of eating him, oftentimes predators lose interest.

VIRGINIA OPOSSUM

FUN FACT!
Despite its slimy appearance, snake skin is hard and dry, like our toe nails.

Why do snakes shed their skin?

Just like a person can't fit into the same pair of pants his entire life, snakes can't fit into the same skin. Unlike human skin, snake skin doesn't grow when the serpent does. Instead, snakes shed their skin every few weeks or months, so they can continue to grow throughout their lives.

Why Are Snakes' Tongues Forked?

It's the closest things snakes have to surround sound—or surround smell. A snake's forked tongue is like a nose that senses chemicals in the air. If a snake identifies a certain chemical balance, it knows to follow its tongue to its prey.

GRAY WOLVES

Why Do Wolves Move In Packs?

Wolves are super social animals who work together to live as comfortably as possible. Wolf packs hunt, travel and raise pups together. A pack is one big happy family—literally. Most of the time, all the members of a pack are related by blood.

Why do wolves sometimes show their teeth?

That way, everyone knows they've got them. Wolves pull their ears back and bare their teeth as a sign of aggression. When other animals see those pearly whites, they know to stay away.

Why Do Wolves Howl?

Howls help wolves communicate. Wolves might howl to warn neighboring packs to stay away or to lead one of their own back home. If a member of one pack howls too close to another, the wolves will sometimes find each other and fight for territory.

FUN FACT!
Lone wolves, who were kicked out of their packs, rarely howl.

Why do beavers like to gnaw on wood?

Wood and veggies are beavers' main source of food, not to mention one of their favorite meals. So when you see a beaver munching on a log, he's enjoying a delicious, nutritious snack. But beavers can't eat all the wood they find. They need logs for building, too. They use them to create their elaborate houses, which are called dams. Can you imagine living in a home made of your favorite food? Yum!

NORTH AMERICAN BEAVER

Why do beavers' tails look like paddles?

Beavers' tails are huge! As big as 16 inches long and 7 inches wide, they come in handy for just about everything you could imagine. Beavers use their tails to regulate their body temperature, hold dam-building materials, swim and prop themselves up. Beavers also slap their tails against the water to warn their friends of danger. Despite what some people think, beavers don't use their thick tails to plaster their dams.

Why do beavers build wooden dams?

Beavers are like the engineers of the animal kingdom. These incredibly smart, hardworking critters build dams, which they live in to protect themselves, raise their young and hunt for food, especially during winter months when river water is frozen. Beavers use tree branches, rocks and mud to make their dams sturdy and waterproof. Why don't other animals do the same? They aren't as resourceful.

THE RAINFO

It's awfully wet!

Tropical rainforests get more than 70 inches of rainfall each year! All that water helps lots of plants grow, from colorful flowers to enormous trees. The forests can get pretty big, too. The Amazon River Basin forest covers nearly six million square miles—almost twice the size of Australia! But don't be fooled: Rainforests take up only 6 percent of Earth's land. Still, that tiny bit of land is home to more than half the world's wildlife, which live in the forest's four layers— emergent, canopy, understory and floor. From harpy eagles to tree frogs to alligators, rainforest animals are some of the most diverse, unusual and brightly hued on the planet!

REST

Home to bright-billed toucans and red-eyed frogs, this habitat has an animal for each color of the rainbow.

FUN FACT!
Sometimes trees here are so close together it takes rain 10 minutes to hit the ground!

Key Features

1. Located along or near the equator

2. Temperatures usually between 70°F and 95°F

3. Averages more than 70 inches of rainfall a year

4. Sunny at the top but dark at the bottom

5. All of its trees keep their leaves year-round

Why Do Toucans Have Such Large Beaks?

The tropical bird's big bill, which is packed with blood vessels, keeps toucans cool on hot days. Heat heads to the bill, then out of the body. The bill also keeps toucans warm. It's just like a thermostat!

TOCO TOUCAN

INDIAN PEACOCK

Why do peacocks spread their feathers?

Just like people might dress up for a date, male peacocks flash their colorful blue and purple feathers to help them attract mates. It works better than a suit and tie ever could.

Why are rainforest animals so colorful?

Filled with lush vegetation and vibrant flowers, the rainforest is as colorful as a 64-pack of crayons. From blue macaws to orange frogs, rainforest animals use their patterns to blend into their surroundings. Monkeys match tree bark, big dark cats blend into the shadows and colorful birds match the fruit and flowers in the trees. There, animals with bold patterns blend right in.

HARPY EAGLE

FUN FACT!
Not all rainforest animals are bright and colorful! Take the harpy eagle, for example—they're gray.

Why Do Parrots Talk?

Parrots talk because they're social animals who love to make noise. Because people don't learn to speak parrot, parrots learn to speak people! They imitate language for attention and interaction, but when you hear parrots "talk," they're not really speaking like a person would. For example, they might be able to say, "Mack want a cracker" if they've heard the phrase, but they can't answer questions uniquely or string sentences together. Parrots can only imitate what they've heard.

Macaws are parrots. Can you guess which other birds are, too?

A) Woodpeckers

B) Cockatoos

C) Penguins

Check your answers on page 176!

Stop copying me!

Stop copying me!

Stop copying me!

DID YOU KNOW?
Even though all macaws are parrots, not all parrots are macaws. Why? Macaw is a kind of parrot!

BRAZILIAN ARMADILLO

Why do armadillos roll into balls?

Imagine trying to break a bowling ball. It'd be very difficult, and you'd likely get hurt in the process! With tough plates of armor covering their bodies, armadillos are almost as impenetrable, especially when they roll into tight balls. The stealthy move is an extremely effective defense mechanism, but it only works for some species, like the Brazilian armadillo. Other types can't roll their bodies up.

Why do lemurs have stripes on their tails?

Unlike most animals, lemurs' coloration isn't meant to help them blend into their surroundings. Instead, their black-and-white tails are designed to help them stand out amongst vegetation and other animals! The rings make it easier for the bright-eyed animals to locate each other in the dark, shaded rainforest. Each lemur's tail has 12 or 13 white stripes, 13 or 14 black stripes and a black tip.

RING-TAILED LEMUR

BINTURONG

Why do some animals smell funny?

Although most animals don't smell as stinky as skunks, each one has its own unique scent that helps it communicate with both friends and foes. Take binturongs, or bearcats, for example. They use their distinct smell to mark their territory and find mates. So what's their scent like? Nothing close to a skunk's! To humans, binturongs smell similar to buttered popcorn.

Why Do Macaws Eat Clay?

When pickings are slim, macaws aren't picky. They'll scour the forest for fruit and eat the seeds from anything they can find—even poisonous plants. The birds counter the sometimes toxic seeds with clay, which helps them eliminate harmful substances from their bodies.

MACAWS

Why do birds have feathers?

All birds have feathers—and for a good reason! Feathers keep them warm and help them fly. Some birds even use the colors of their feathers as camouflage or to attract mates.

DID YOU KNOW?
Macaws are the biggest parrots out there. Their wingspan can stretch more than 4 feet!

AUSTRALIAN RAINBOW LORIKEET

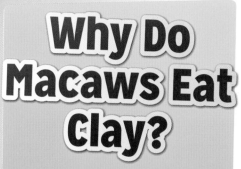

FUN FACT!
Ancient Greeks called hippos "river horses" because of the animal's love of water.

LEOPARD

Why aren't big cats scared of water?

Most house cats are scared of water because their only experience with it is unpleasant. For example, house cats are sometimes disciplined with spray bottles. But big cats, such as leopards, aren't scared of water because it benefits them. In water, they can hunt and stay cool.

Why Do Hippos Spend So Much Time In The Water?

Pygmy hippos love water so much it's like they wish they were fish! Turns out, they might have been—scientists think their closest living relatives are whales and dolphins. With that comes a ton of tricks. Their eyes, ears and nostrils are on the top of their heads, so they can breathe while in water. Hippos also have covers on their eyes like goggles and can hold their breath for more than five minutes at a time! Hippos can even sleep in water thanks to a reflex that bobs them up for air.

COMMON HIPPOPOTAM

Why Do Tree Frogs Have Red Eyes?

Flashy colors catch our attention, and the same is true with animals. Red-eyed tree frogs bat their eyes in the face of predators, shocking potential attackers with vibrant color. When the overstimulated predator stops to think twice about his meal choice, the frog has a chance to escape. But the red-eyed tree frog doesn't always want its peepers to stun the animals around it. When it sleeps, the tree frog closes its eyes and hides its bright orange feet to better blend in with the green foliage of the forest treetops.

Frogs aren't born as frogs. Do you know what hatches from a frog egg?

A) A worm

B) A caterpillar

C) A tadpole

Check your answers on page 176!

RED-EYED TREE FROG

FUN FACT!
Red-eyed tree frogs, also called red-eyed leaf frogs, are about the size of a teacup.

BLUE POISON DART FROG

FUN FACT!
Blue poison dart frogs make soft buzzing noises when they call to their mates.

Why Do Frogs Ribbit?

Like each human has a unique voice, each frog has its own special sound. Some whistle, while others peep, cluck or grunt. The noise we're most familiar with, however, is by far the ribbet. Males croak to attract female frogs and to keep competing males off their turf.

Why do frogs have such long tongues?

Well, an amphibian's gotta eat! Frogs' tongues help them do just that. Frogs love fly meat, but those little guys aren't the easiest insects to nab. Because flies and other winged insects are so quick, frogs have to be even quicker. That, or go without eating. Because frogs can't fly like their prey, they have long, sticky tongues that make catching lunch much easier than it would be otherwise.

GREEN TREE FROG

Why do toads have warts all over them?

The bumps and lumps you see all over toads are actually pockets of poison that look—and taste—gross to amphibian-eating predators, such as snakes and birds. So although they might not look very glamorous, toads' warts protect them. But it's toad-ally unfair to blame these little guys for the warts that people sometimes get on their hands and feet. Those can only be passed from person to person.

RED-SPOTTED TOAD

Why do frogs puff up when they croak?

By puffing themselves up, frogs can create a natural megaphone that resonates their croaks. As a result, noises that come from their tightly stretched vocal cords sound even louder. This comes in handy in the rainforest, where just about every frog can blend into its surroundings. How else would a frog find its brothers and sisters or its future spouse? Good thing they can puff up, huh?

RED-EYED TREE FROG

THE RAINFOREST

GIANT PANDA

DID YOU KNOW?
One way to help endangered animals is to recycle. That way, forests stay put!

Why Are Some Species Endangered?

Like orangutans, poisonous dart frogs and many other species in the world's rainforests, pandas are an **endangered** species, with only about 1,600 left in the wild. Pandas were once common in China, but many of their homes were overtaken by development, and the big bears were pushed into smaller, less livable habitats. Like other endangered species, pandas are poached, or hunted illegally. If the number of pandas in the wild continues to decline, the animal could disappear completely.

Why do pandas eat so much bamboo?

If you think your school lunch menu is boring, you'd hate a panda's diet. They eat leaves, stems and bamboo, which have almost no nutritional value. It'd be like eating celery and nothing else! To get energy, pandas eat more than 80 pounds of bamboo every day. That's the weight of an average 10-year-old boy!

SOUND IT OUT!

Endangered (en-DAYN-jerd)

Endangered means at risk of extinction. When an animal goes extinct, there are none left in the world. For example, dinosaurs are extinct.

Why Do Monkeys' And Apes' Arms Drag On The Ground?

Most monkeys and apes have incredibly long arms with sturdy, flexible shoulders that allow them to swing from tree to tree with little effort. (There's a reason those things on the playground are called monkey bars!) Because of the sheer length of their limbs, primates' arms sometimes drag on the ground. Luckily, they don't have to worry about washing their hands.

Orangutans are a lot like people. Which feature is most similar?

A Our eyes

B Our hair

C Our hands

Check your answers on page 176!

FUN FACT!
Orangutans love hanging out—they spend about 90 percent of their lives in the trees of the rainforest.

"Your nails are pretty dirty."

"So's the rest of him!"

ORANGUTANS

MANDRILL

Why do mandrills have such colorful faces?

Mandrills are the largest species of monkey, and their bright red and blue faces make them easy to recognize. But that's only part of the reason why they have such bright faces—male mandrills also use their markings to attract mates. Their faces become even more colorful when they get excited. Some mandrills' faces are brighter than others, too. The strongest mandrills have the brightest faces.

Why do monkeys like to eat bananas?

Monkeys and bananas have something important in common: their homes! Bananas grow in the same tropical areas monkeys live, making the yellow fruit an obvious snack. Conveniently packaged, bananas offer monkeys lots of nutrients and flavor. But the bananas we eat are different than the ones monkeys consume in the wild. The ones you get at a store have more sugar and calories so they are bad for monkeys' teeth.

CRAB-EATING MACAQUE

CHIMPANZEE

Why do monkeys throw their poop?

Monkeys don't have sports to turn to when they're bored like we do. Instead, they throw poop! Monkeys throw poop for other reasons, too. Just about any reason, really—like when they feel angry, feisty or silly. Some people think throwing poop is a monkey's way of entertaining his peers. Regardless of the reason, scientists agree on one thing: Throwing poop is a sign of smarts. But that doesn't mean you should do it!

Why Are Spider Monkeys Named After A Bug?

Wouldn't it be nice to have an extra hand when you're lugging around a bookbag, a lunch sack and who knows what else? Although spider monkeys don't technically have a third arm, they have a tail that doubles as one! Their tails are **prehensile**, which means they can grab things and move objects. Spider monkeys got their name in part thanks to those strong, able tails, which help them navigate treetops, swinging from branch to branch from arm to leg to tail. Oftentimes, they grab different branches with each of their limbs and tails, which look quite spiderlike.

SOUND IT OUT!

Prehensile
(pree-HEN-sill)

Prehensile means "capable of grasping," and it's a word that applies to different parts of different animals. Spider monkeys have prehensile tails, tapirs have prehensile noses and giraffes have prehensile tongues.

"Ssstay away, ssstranger."

FUN FACT!
Snakes don't hiss to communicate with their own kind. In fact, they prefer to be alone.

AMAZON TREE BOA

Why do snakes sometimes hiss?

Although some snakes are deadly, most are small and harmless. So instead of venom, these little guys use their tongues to scare predators. Hissing gives the impression of a bigger, more dangerous snake—because big snakes hiss, too! In the end, it's a scare tactic designed to keep snakes safe.

Why Are Snakes Able To Climb Trees?

Without arms and legs, you'd think climbing would be hard for snakes, but the opposite is true. Snakes use their muscular bodies to squeeze their way up rough-surfaced trees. In addition to pushing against surfaces with more than nine times their body weight, snakes use their scales to get a great grip. By angling their scales outward, snakes can dig into the bark's rough surface, creating more friction and making climbing easier.

Why Do Sloths Move So Slowly?

Exercise is easy if you've got lots of muscle. But if you don't, you're in the same boat as a sloth. Sloths have about half as much muscle as other animals of the same size and weight. That, coupled with a slow metabolism, makes walking strenuous and running even harder. So sluggish sloths only move when necessary—even then creeping slowly, moving about 41 yards per day, which is less than half the length of a football field. When in danger, sloths can move faster and farther, but it wears them out big time!

DID YOU KNOW?
Sloths spend most of their time sleeping. You'll find them napping 20 hours per day!

FUN FACT!
Like owls, sloths can turn their heads almost all the way around—when the lazy guys feel like it, that is!

Can you guess just how slow sloths are? They're so sluggish that:

A snails outrun them

B fossils form faster

C algae grows on them

Check your answers on page 176!

THREE-TOED SLOTH

Why Do Sloths Smile?

With an ever-present smile on his face, the sloth might seem like the happiest animal on the planet. But don't be fooled! That's just how sloths' mouths are shaped. We have no way of knowing how they actually feel.

Why do piranhas have teeth?

Can you imagine trying to eat a hamburger without chompers? It wouldn't be easy! Like us, piranhas are meat-eaters that need teeth to chew their food. Piranhas' razor sharp teeth are similar to sharks' and are perfect for biting into fleshy insects, fish and worms.

DID YOU KNOW?
Piranhas have scary-looking teeth, but they also use another tactic to intimidate other species: They bark.

Why do chameleons change color?

Chameleons only change color to blend into their surroundings, right? Wrong! Scientists have found that the reptiles change color for a number of reasons: to blend in, to cool down and to communicate, which some studies suggest was the reason chameleons learned the trick in the first place. Instead of making noise, they speak with colors, and different patterns mean different things.

YEMEN CHAMELEON

Why do anteaters have such long noses?

GIANT ANTEATER

It'd be tough to drink out of a fast food cup without a straw, just like it would be hard to probe an anthill without a long, tube-like nose. Anteaters stick their skinny snouts into anthills to check out their prospective dinners. If they like what they smell, they stick their extra long tongues—which can reach up to 2 feet in length—into the holes and lap up the yummy insects living inside. Slurrrrrrrrp!

Why are crocodiles such good swimmers?

With big, bulky bodies, crocodiles might not look like they can navigate the water, but the aquatic reptiles can swim faster than 10 miles per hour! That's not top speed in the animal kingdom, but it's still an impressive feat for the nearly 2,000-pound creatures. Their huge, powerful tails propel them forward, while their feet squish against their bodies to give them the aquatic skills of a fish.

SALTWATER CROCODILE

Why Do Gorillas Beat Their Chests?

You might see a winning athlete do the same thing for the same reason: victory! When a gorilla wins a fight, he pounds his chest to rub the triumph in. It's his way of saying, "Nanner nanner boo boo!" A signal of general dominance, gorillas also beat their chests when challenged by younger gorillas or when requesting their families to follow them.

DID YOU KNOW?
Gorillas don't have a taste for meat. Instead, their diet is mainly vegetarian. They like to eat stems, bamboo shoots, fruits and sometimes ants or termites.

LOWLAND GORILLA

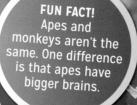

FUN FACT!
Apes and monkeys aren't the same. One difference is that apes have bigger brains.

My wife Suzi and I visit Rwanda every year. Sue snapped this photo of an endangered mountain gorilla in 2014.

Why do some types of gorillas have long hair?

Long hair can make a gorilla's life easier. Some lowland gorillas live in warm western Africa, but other subspecies, such as mountain gorillas, live in colder mountain ranges in the middle of the continent. They have longer hair and larger bodies to help them endure the chilly temperatures.

THE OCEAN

The wettest part of the world is filled with tons and tons of wonderfully wild animals!

Surf's Up!

The ocean is the world's largest habitat, and it takes up 71 percent of the Earth! There are three major oceans—the Pacific, the Atlantic and the Indian—but they all touch, despite differences in their currents and temperatures. As many as one million unique species live in the ocean's 320 million cubic miles. There are also three zones in each ocean—surface, twilight and deep ocean—and each zone has its own habitat and wildlife. Animals in the surface zone of the Pacific, such as bottlenose dolphins, are different from the wildlife in deepest part of the Atlantic, such as anglerfish, but each animal is perfectly adapted to thrive in its water-filled world.

FUN FACT!
The colorful coral that fills reefs might look like a plant, but it's really an animal!

Key Features

1. Filled with lots of salty water

2. All oceans are connected

3. Has an average depth of 2 miles

4. Surrounds all of the Earth's land

5. Has three zones: surface, twilight and deep

FUN FACT!
Dolphins catch serious air! They've been known to jump up to 16 feet out of the water.

Why are dolphins light on one side and dark on the other?

Dolphins' skin tone is like a disguise that helps them swim in secret. When sharks swim above them, dolphins' gray tops help them blend into the ocean floor. When dolphins are swimming above sharks, their white stomachs help them disappear into the ocean's surface.

While filming for *Jack Hanna's Into the Wild*, my wife Sue and I assisted with a dolphin training at the Dolphin Academy in Curacao. While on the island, we also participated in a dolphin therapy session for disabled children and adults.

Why Do Dolphins Jump Out Of The Water?

Scientist aren't 100 percent sure why dolphins jump, but they have a few ideas. Some scientists think dolphins leap to save energy or to get a good view of what's in the distance. Other researchers think jumping might be a way for dolphins to communicate or to clean themselves. But, some experts think dolphins bound for one of the same reasons we do: for fun!

Why Are Orcas Sometimes Called "Killer Whales?"

They might look nice and friendly, but with three-inch-long locking teeth and big brains, orcas are incredibly smart predators that rule the ocean. In fact, they're so smart they develop hunting strategies with their brothers and sisters depending on where they are and what they want to eat. Orcas have been known to coordinate attacks on seals, sea lions and even whales.

ORCA

**Orcas are huge!
Can you guess about
how long they are?**

A Almost as long as a car

B Almost as long as a bus

C Almost as long as a jet

Check your answers
on page 176!

FUN FACT!
Despite their
nickname, orcas belong
to the dolphin family. With
black backs and white
tummies, they camouflage
themselves just like
their cousins!

Why Are Blue Whales So Big?

Whales are the biggest animals on the planet. The blue whale is about 85 feet long and weighs around 106 tons. That's as long as a basketball court and as heavy as 30 elephants! Their size has to do with how they eat and where they live. Because whales don't have to support their weight on legs like we do, they can get pretty big. Plus, they have huge mouths that allow them to catch lots of food every time they eat.

FIN WHALE

Why do whales and dolphins have those holes on their heads?

Those things are called blowholes. Instead of gills, whales and dolphins have lungs, which means their blowholes are kind of like noses! Whales and dolphins use them to breathe every time they come up to the water's surface for air.

Why do whales like singing so much?

Some of the smartest people in the world aren't sure why some whales, such as humpbacks, sing. But here's what we do know: Only male whales sing. Some scientists think the songs are meant to attract or excite female whales. Another theory is that the songs are used to help male whales keep space between them or to show off their social status. In the end, though, no one's entirely sure. But it sure sounds cool!

Why do some whales have white crust on them?

HUMPBACK WHALE

That white crust is actually a small neighborhood built by barnacles. Barnacles are little, shelled animals that latch onto a surface for life and survive by catching food with their long, feathery legs. For a hungry barnacle, a whale's head is a great place to be. When that whale swims through a swarm of plankton for food, the barnacle gets a free meal. Plus, they get to see more of the ocean! It's like living on a giant underwater cruise ship!

Why are most whales' voices so loud?

When you talk to your mom from a different room, you have to speak up. Imagine trying to hear her from all the way across the ocean! You would have to get pretty loud, too. Whales are the loudest animals on the planet for just that reason: They have to communicate across huge distances. Whales' voices can travel thousands and thousands of miles, so they'll never need to be asked to speak up!

FUN FACT! Sometimes, jellyfish sting accidentally, so be careful not to touch them!

Why do jellyfish sting other animals?

Jellyfish sting to catch prey and protect themselves. Like snakes, jellyfish are venomous and will throw out a tentacle if they feel threatened. They have tiny cells on their flowy limbs that paralyze victims, making meals and escapes pretty easy.

SOUND IT OUT!

Bioluminescence (bi-oh-loo-muh-NEH-sents)

Bioluminescence means "the emission of light from living organisms." Bioluminescence is pretty rare, but it's most common in marine animals. Certain squids, octopuses and jellyfish are bioluminescent. But some creatures above the water are, too. If you're having trouble imagining an animal with a built-in flashlight, just think about fireflies. They've mastered it!

Why Do Jellyfish Glow?

Not all jellyfish glow, but most of them look like they do! Their see-through bodies catch light like glass, resulting in pretty colors. But the jellyfish that truly glow do so thanks to special proteins in their biological makeup. When animals glow it's called **bioluminescence**.

Some jellyfish are dangerous. Which of these is most deadly?

A) **The Box Jellyfish**

B) **The Purple Jellyfish**

C) **The Moon Jellyfish**

Check your answers on page 176!

SIAMESE FIGHTING BETTA FISH

FUN FACT!
Some fish, like different kinds of bettas, can live in salt and fresh waters!

Why Can Some Fish Live In Salt Water While Others Can't?

If you have red hair and light skin, you probably wouldn't do well in Ecuador. You'd get sunburnt! Similarly, if you're a freshwater fish, you wouldn't do well in the ocean. It's too salty! Freshwater fish can regulate the salt in their bodies, so they're primed for saltless surroundings. But fish that live in the ocean are made to push extra salt out. Without the right mechanism for the environment, fish would struggle to survive.

Why do starfish wash ashore?

They don't have much of a choice. Given their name, you might think starfish can swim. But think again! Starfish use the suction cups on their arms to creep and crawl through the ocean from surface to surface. If the ocean current is strong enough, starfish can't control where they end up—which means a big wave could wash them right onto the beach!

Why do some starfish look like they're missing arms?

Because they are! Sometimes starfish decide they'd rather lose an arm than their whole life! Losing limbs keeps starfish safe. Unlike people, when a starfish loses an arm, it can grow it back in about a year. So if a crab clamps onto it, a starfish would much rather break off their own arm than lose their whole body. Starfish also lose arms when they get too hot. Because their center is much cooler than their arms, doing this can help the starfish survive in waters that are too warm.

DID YOU KNOW?
Starfish, or sea stars, use water instead of blood to pump nutrients through their bodies.

BLOOD PARROT

Why Don't Fish Sink When They Sleep?

If you've ever worn a life jacket, you know they make it nearly impossible to sink. Most fish have natural life jackets inside their tummies called swim bladders. Swim bladders keep fish afloat all the time—even when they sleep. And because they can control the amount of gas in their swim bladders, they can keep themselves from constantly floating on top of the water.

Can you guess which aquatic animals don't have a swim bladder?

A Blood Parrots

B Hammerhead Sharks

C Puffer Fish

Check your answers on page 176!

Why don't fish have any arms or legs?

Even olympian Michael Phelps can't swim as well as a fish. With humans' gangly arms and legs, our bodies aren't exactly built for an underwater life. Fish, like the Blue Tang fish, on the other hand, don't have hands (or feet), so their sleek bodies move effortlessly through the water. Not only is the lack of limbs efficient for swimming, it's also logical. Think about it: Fish don't need to pick anything up or walk anywhere, anyway!

BLUE TANG FISH

Why doesn't water hurt fish's eyes?

Does the oxygen around you hurt your eyes? Of course not! Just like we don't mind getting air in our eyeballs, fish, like the longspine squirrelfish, don't mind getting salty ocean water in theirs. It doesn't hurt them because their eyes have adapted to their underwater environment. They're so used to it that they don't even need eyelids. And that's good because there wouldn't be enough goggles in the world for every aquatic animal to wear!

LONGSPINE SQUIRRELFISH

Why do some fish clean other fish?

If your clothes and toys were all made of delicious fudge, wouldn't you be more interested in cleaning your room? For cleaner fish, whose favorite food is dead skin with a side of parasites, the reward they get for cleaning their fellow fish is a delicious meal and a full stomach. The fish they feed off of don't mind because, hey, they're getting a free cleaning out of the deal!

MORAY EEL

Why Do Fish Swim In Groups?

Fish travel in groups, which are called
schools, for many reasons. Moving in
schools helps fish find dinner faster
and keeps them safe from predators
who might want to turn them into
lunch. Swimming in schools also makes
traveling easier. In schools, fish like the
bigeye move in perfect motion—just like
in a synchronized swimming routine—
which helps them save energy.

COMMON BIG EYE FISH

LIONFISH

Why Don't Fish Drown?

Fish need oxygen to survive, but instead of coming to the surface of the water for air, most fish use their gills to take in dissolved oxygen from the water. Because they don't have lungs, the oxygen goes right into their bloodstreams. Fish like the lionfish use their gills to push unwanted water out of their bodies, so they never have to worry about drowning. But fish are in trouble if the water they live in doesn't have enough oxygen. For example, if the water gets too hot, the right amount of air can't dissolve into the water—which means their gills won't help them.

DID YOU KNOW?
Lionfish are poisonous, but they don't use their poison to catch food—they use it to keep from becoming a meal! But don't touch them. Lionfish venom is painful.

FUN FACT! Seahorses mate differently than most animals: The males get pregnant!

Why do seahorses look like that?

Seahorses are fish, but they sure don't look like it! They have the tail of a monkey and the pouch of a kangaroo, along with a face that looks like it was created by Dr. Seuss. Scientists believe seahorses look the way they do because of the way they prefer to catch food: quickly and by surprise.

FUN FACT!
Sea otters don't just float. They can dive as deep as 330 feet when they're looking for food!

COMMON SEA OTTERS

Why Do Sea Otters Hold Hands?

Just like you might hold hands with someone while floating down the lazy river at your favorite water park (my favorite is Zoombezi Bay, right next to the Columbus Zoo!), sea otters hold hands so they don't lose their family members while napping on the water. Sometimes only a few sea otters link hands, while other times as many as 100 hang on at once! The otters hold hands sometimes when they're awake, too. That way, they won't float away from their friends while they're eating a delicious meal of clams and mussels.

DID YOU KNOW?
When sea otters float together in those interlocked groups, it's called rafting. To us, though, it looks like holding hands.

GIANT OCTOPUS

FUN FACT!
Some octopuses will collect shells to keep outside their homes for decoration.

Why Do Octopuses Have So Many Tentacles?

Octopuses have eight tentacles because eight hands are better than two! Each tentacle has its own bit of brain, making octopuses extremely smart animals. The tentacles each have their own job, too, and each can be busy at the same time. Four tentacles are used for movement, and four are used for feeding and handling objects.

Why do some octopuses squirt out ink?

Have you ever seen a magic show? If so, you know magicians sometimes disappear. Octopuses use their ink to do the same thing! When a predator comes after them, octopuses spray their ink and swim away as the dark cloud disorients their attacker. But the ink does more than just hide the octopus. It also harms enemies by irritating their eyes and affecting their senses of smell and taste.

COMMON OCTOPUS

Why do octopuses have suction cups on their tentacles?

Sometimes, it's hard to pick up a wet shampoo bottle without dropping it. Now imagine living underwater! It'd make grabbing things even tougher. An octopus has suction cups on its tentacles for just that reason. They make picking things up like food and rocks much easier. Without the suction cups, an octopus's arms would be a lot less handy.

COMMON CRAB

Why do crabs always seem to walk sideways?

People can walk sideways, too, but we usually don't. The same goes for crabs—but opposite. Crabs can walk forward, but only in a slow shuffle, so they usually don't. That'd be a waste of time! Because crabs' knees only bend sideways (instead of forward and backward like ours), stepping straight ahead is tough for them. Walking the way they do—sideways—is just easier!

Why are some eels electric?

Electric eels use their charge to stun prey and scare away predators. Their bodies are covered with tiny cells called electrolytes that store power like batteries. And, boy, are they effective! An electric eel's charge is so strong it's been known to knock a horse off its feet. Why aren't all eels electric? Because electric eels aren't eels at all! Even though they look like eels, they are actually closer in nature to catfish.

ELECTRIC EEL

FLYING FISH

Why do flying fish jump out of the water?

It's a bird! It's a plane! No, it's a flying fish! Flying fish can soar out of the water unlike most other species of fish—but they don't do it for fun. Most of the time, these fish jump to escape predators. To avoid becoming swordfish food or a mackerel's lunch, flying fish use their winglike fins to help them soar out of the water. And, they sure are good at it! They've been known to glide more than 650 feet at a time!

Why Are Stingrays Flat?

Stingrays spend a lot of their time on the bottom of the ocean, which is why they're shaped the way they are: It helps them blend in with their favorite places to hang out! Disguised as the ocean floor, stingrays are much safer from sharks and other predators, so they can focus on the better things in life—like eating.

DID YOU KNOW?
The Columbus Zoo and Aquarium (and many other zoos) has an interactive stingray feeding experience that allows guests to get up close and personal with these incredible creatures.

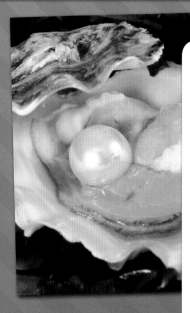

Why are there pearls inside oysters?

When a person gets an eyelash in her eye, it waters; it's the body's natural response to keep eyes clean and vision clear. Oysters have a similar reaction when bits of sand get in their shell. Instead of pushing the sand out, they cover the grain with a mineral to avoid irritation. After a few mineral layers build up, a pearl forms. The longer a piece of sand stays inside an oyster, the bigger pearl it will produce!

Why Do Some Marine Animals Head To The Surface For Air?

Not all underwater animals have gills like fish do. Animals without gills have lungs—just like you!—so they have to get air from above the water's surface. Whales, dolphins and sea turtles all have lungs, which is why we see these guys up top so often!

DID YOU KNOW?
Unlike some land turtles, sea turtles can't pull their heads or legs into their shells.

BLUB
BLUB
BLUB

Sea turtles typically weigh hundreds of pounds. Which of these species is heaviest?

A Kemps Ridley Sea Turtle

B Loggerhead Sea Turtle

C Green Sea Turtle

Check your answers on page 176!

FUN FACT!
On average a sea turtle nest has 110 eggs, but only a few survive to become adults because of predators.

Why Do Sea Turtles Lay Eggs On The Beach?

They couldn't do it in the ocean! Baby sea turtles need air to survive, and they don't have the gills they would need to get it from the water. If a mama turtle laid her eggs at the bottom of the ocean, the baby turtles wouldn't have time to get to the surface for air. Once the turtles hatch on the beach, they follow the light of the moon and head for the ocean water.

Why do fish have scales all over their bodies?

Underneath their scales, fish have extremely soft bodies. You know how walking without shoes sometimes leads you to step on something that hurts your feet? Fish scales are like shoes for a fish's whole body. Scales are really just thin pieces of bone that overlap to form a suit of armor that helps protect fish from the harmful stuff in the underwater world around them.

RAINBOW FISH

Why don't fish have ears like ours? Can they hear?

SENEGAL BICHIR

Fish don't have ears like ours, but they do have ear bones, and they can hear. So why can't we see them? Because tiny fish ears are even smaller than a grain of sand, and they're located inside fish's heads. Fish also have a special sense that helps them detect motion throughout the water. Just as we might hear the footsteps of someone trying to sneak up on us, fish can sense the movement of predators in the water. Good thing!

Why do swordfish have pointy noses?

Swordfish aren't using those spears on their faces to smell! Technically, fish don't have noses at all. And despite what people think, they don't use their swords to poke things. Instead, the nose sword is a handy tool that helps swordfish do everything from swim faster to hunt better. The spear cuts through water, allowing swordfish to move as fast as 50 miles per hour and slash through schools of smaller fish that look tasty.

BLUE MARLIN

REEF SHARK

Why Do Sharks Have So Many Teeth?

Imagine how frustrating it would be for you to lose a tooth every time you ate a sandwich. You'd stop smiling pretty quickly! When sharks munch on their prey, they bite down pretty hard. So hard, in fact, that their teeth sometimes fall out. To fix that, sharks never stop growing teeth, and some species have as many as eight rows. Good thing they don't have to brush!

FUN FACT!
Without their dorsal fins, sharks would have no choice but to swim upside down!

DID YOU KNOW?
As tough as sharks are, they don't have a single bone in their bodies. Instead, sharks are made of cartilage, the same stuff our noses are made of!

Why do sharks swim with one fin out of the water?

Even if you've never seen a real shark, you've probably caught a glimpse of one on TV. Why does the shark always seem to have one fin out of the water? Doesn't that give him away? To us, maybe, but most shark species actually swim stealthily near the bottom or the middle of the ocean. The fin on a shark's back is called the dorsal fin, and it's used for balance. The only reason we see it above the water's surface is because that's the only time we see sharks at all! Most of the time, sharks stay away from the surface all together.

THE POLES

This barren habitat is the polar opposite of what you'd expect: It's crawling with critters!

Key Features

1. Located at the top and bottom of the Earth

2. Covered with ice and snow, not plants

3. Below freezing temperatures

4. Very little darkness during the summer

5. Very little sunlight during the winter

Brrr, it's freezing!

Earth's poles are found at the very top and the very bottom of the world. The Arctic is located at the North Pole, and the Antarctic, which is technically a desert, is located at the South Pole. Characterized by freezing temperatures, snow and ice, polar landscapes aren't lush with plants and flowers. Instead, everything is frozen and white, barring summers up north, when temperatures rise just above freezing. But what these seemingly barren habitats lack in vegetation, they make up for in diverse wildlife—from polar bears in the Arctic to penguins at the other end of the globe.

EMPEROR PENGUINS

Why Do Male Emperor Penguins Sit On Eggs?

Mother penguins are exhausted after laying an egg, so instead of babysitting, they take to the ocean to regain the strength they lost producing their soon-to-be baby bird. While females hunt, males have daycare duty. To protect their eggs from the cold, male penguins balance them on their feet and cover them with their feathered skin. Then, they stay that way for two months without eating or drinking!

Why do penguins slide on their stomachs?

Which would you rather do: Slide down a snow-covered hill full speed ahead or inch down the icy terrain on foot? The first option probably sounds better to both you and a penguin! Penguins sled over ice on their stomachs because it's faster and easier than waddling across the slippery landscape. When they need to get somewhere quickly, penguins take to their tummies.

GENTOO PENGUIN

CHINSTRAP PENGUIN

Why don't penguins live at the North Pole?

Forget what you've seen in soda commercials: Penguins and polar bears aren't neighbors. Penguins live at the South Pole, and polar bears live at the North. With short legs and stubby wings, penguins are vulnerable on land, where they nest with their young. Luckily, their home in the Antarctic has very few predators. If the flightless birds lived at the North Pole, they would be an easy meal for bears, wolves and foxes.

Why do penguins waddle instead of walk?

What's the quickest way to get from one point to another? For a penguin, it's to waddle! Scientists aren't totally sure why penguins waddle, but most agree that it's the best way for the little guys to get around. With such short legs, it'd be hard for them to put one foot in front of the other. Instead, they sway to save energy and gain momentum. Although they might walk weirdly, those little legs turn into useful rudders in the water.

ADELIE PENGUIN

GENTOO PENGUIN

FUN FACT!
Gentoo penguins dive into the water as many as 450 times per day to search for food.

Why can't penguins fly like other birds?

Like ostriches and roadrunners, penguins have short, stubby wings that aren't made for flying. And even if they were, their pudgy bodies would be a chore to carry through the sky! Luckily, penguins are world-class swimmers, so they can easily navigate icy waters to escape their enemies and catch food without lifting off the ground.

Why do penguins have wings if they can't fly?

Penguin wings might not do much above sea level, but below water, the hard, narrow flippers are a bird's best friend! They help the aquatic birds propel themselves through the water. Why can't other birds swim? Their large, flexible made-for-flying wings would be useless in the water. It'd be like using a piece of paper as a paddle!

Why Are Penguins Black And White?

If you were wearing a tuxedo in the snow you might stick out, but in the Antarctic, the black-and-white look helps both male and female penguins blend in. The coloration is called countershading, and it helps camouflage the birds to protect them from the seals and sharks that live in the water. From above, their black backs blend into the ocean floor, and from below, their white tummies look one with the sky. Sound familiar? They share the strategy with dolphins.

Why Do Polar Bears Spend So Much Time In The Water?

With black skin, white fur and a thick layer of fat, polar bears are great at staying warm. In fact, they're almost too good at it! One reason polar bears take to the water is to cool down when they get too hot. A polar bear might go for a swim after a lot of exercise on a warm day.

DID YOU KNOW? Polar bear fur isn't actually white! It just looks that way. The hairs are pigment free, which means they don't have color.

Why do polar bears have white fur but black skin?

Polar bears' white coats are great for camouflage, but the black skin they have underneath is even more useful. It helps them soak up the sun's rays. In freezing weather, staying warm is what's most important.

POLAR BEARS

Why do polar bears fight each other?

There's only one way to get better: practice, practice, practice. Polar bears know that, too. That's what they're doing when they spar with each other. Instead of fighting, the bears are actually playing to practice hunting and to determine the strongest bears in the bunch.

ATLANTIC PUFFIN

"Who are you calling big mouth?!"

DID YOU KNOW?
A puffin's beak gets bigger as the bird ages, which is great for hunting. The bigger the beak, the more fish a puffin can catch at once. Usually, the bird can catch about 10 fish at a time.

Why Do Puffins Have Such Pretty Beaks?

Puffins look kind of like penguins, but their colorful beaks give their identities away. Marked with orange, yellow, black and white, their beaks have earned them the nickname "sea parrot." Because their beaks are brightest during the spring, scientists think puffins use them to look great for potential mates.

FUN FACT!
Puffins are one of the smallest seabirds out there. They're only about 10 inches tall!

Why do puffins dive in the water?

Penguins aren't the only water bird on the ice block. Puffins are well-adapted to the sea, too. They have waterproof feathers that keeps them warm as they hunt for their main food source: fish. They dive into the water and scoop as many as they can into their mouths. Puffins also drink saltwater, something people can't do.

SIBERIAN HUSKY

Why Do Huskies Have Such Bright Blue Eyes?

Actually, Huskies' eyes can be any color. Just like a person's, a Husky's eye color depends on the traits his parents passed down. Although it's common for Huskies to have blue eyes, some have brown, green or hazel eyes. Additionally, it's not unusual to see a Husky with two different colored eyes or with one eye that's two different colors.

FUN FACT!
Most northern snow dogs are Siberian Huskies or Alaskan Malamutes.

Why does an Arctic fox's fur change color?

Believe it or not, the North Pole, where Arctic foxes live, isn't always snow-covered. In the summer, though it's still cold, most of the snow melts and temperatures rise just above freezing. As the terrain changes color, so do Arctic foxes! Turning brown helps the foxes blend into their summer environments, which makes it easier for them to hide while they hunt for food and evade predators.

ARCTIC FOX

SNOWY OWL

Why aren't there any snakes or lizards at the North and South Poles?

Snakes, lizards and other reptiles are cold-blooded, which means they rely on their environments for heat. In places without much heat—such as the Arctic and the Antarctic—that's not a desirable trait. The frigid habitat would turn snakes into snake-sicles! Instead, the cold habitat is dominated by warm-blooded types, like the snowy owl.

Why do narwhals have those long horns?

Scientists have debated the purpose of a narwhal's tusk for years, but no one's sure of its real purpose. One thing they do know, however, is that only male narwhals have them. Because the trait is unique to males, some researchers think they use the horn to fight for females or territory. Others believe they use the horn to break ice, hunt, dig and seek out differences in the environment—but these theories are unproven.

NARWHALS

Why Do Reindeer Click When They Walk?

Reindeer paws go click, click, click, but not because they're up on the rooftop! Reindeer click when they walk because their tendons, the cords inside their feet that connect bones to each other, stretch across their bones.

Reindeer are polar animals. Which pole do they call home?

A The North Pole

B The South Pole

C Both Poles

Check your answers on page 176!

DID YOU KNOW?
Scientists disagree about whether reindeer and caribou are the same animal. Most people use the terms interchangeably!

ARCTIC REINDEER

Why do reindeer shed their antlers?

To grow new ones! Just like people lose their baby teeth, reindeer lose their antlers to make room for new ones. The process is called **regeneration**. Instead of happening once in a lifetime, regeneration occurs once per year—that's how often reindeer grow new antlers. If they didn't shed their old antlers, they'd have too many pairs and no place to put them.

SOUND IT OUT!

Regeneration (ree-jenn-err-A-shun)

The renewal or restoration of a body part, either after injury or as part of a normal growth process, is called regeneration. Reindeer growing new antlers, starfish growing new arms or lizards growing new tails are all examples of regeneration.

Why Do Reindeer Antlers Look So Soft?

If you've ever seen a pair of reindeer antlers up close and personal, you know they look like they're covered in soft fabric. In fact, scientists call the period of time when antlers grow "velvet." When antlers grow, they're covered in a thin, fuzzy skin that makes them look velvety. When the antlers are fully grown, they become as hard as bone. Later, they fall off, and the process starts over again.

ELK

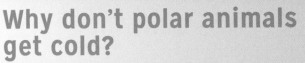

Why don't polar animals get cold?

Because they are warm-blooded, polar animals can make their own heat—but it's always leaving their bodies. To back up their built-in thermostats, the animals have thick layers of fat called blubber to trap in body heat. Fish have special adaptations, too. Their blood is filled with proteins that keep it from freezing solid. The antifreeze works so well that food engineers copied the proteins and use them in ice cream.

BELUGA WHALE

Why would animals want to live somewhere so cold?

Just like desert animals would struggle to survive in the poles, polar animals wouldn't last long under the beating sun of the desert. Their bodies don't lend themselves to cooling down easily. For example, an Arctic hare's short, thick fur would be smothering in high temperatures! Most polar animals have adapted to the weather so well that they don't even get cold. In fact, sometimes they get too hot!

ARCTIC HARE

Why don't polar animals have frozen hair after they go swimming?

Water freezes awfully fast at the poles. Can you imagine wearing a wardrobe of ice? It wouldn't be cool! Luckily for most polar animals, natural oils keep their fur from matting to their bodies and turning to ice after a dip. Without the oils, the animals wouldn't be as fortunate: Their hair would freeze fairly quickly!

POLAR BEAR

Why Are Most Polar Animals White?

In the usually snowy Arctic, being white is kind of like being invisible. And when you're trying to avoid becoming an Arctic wolf's dinner, being hard to see is a huge plus! The camouflage helps animals hide in their surroundings, whether they're hunting for food or hoping to avoid becoming it.

SNOWY OWL

FUN FACT! Walruses can slow their heartbeats to survive cold, polar temperatures.

ATLANTIC WALRUS

Why Do Walruses Have Mustaches?

It'd take a huge razor to shave off those 'staches! Walrus whiskers are thick, extremely sensitive tools they use for hunting. Their mustaches help them search the dark ocean floor for food.

DID YOU KNOW?
Atlantic walruses live in coastal areas from northeastern Canada to Greenland, while Pacific walruses live along the coasts of northern Russia and Alaska.

Why do walruses have such long tusks?

Walruses' tusks never stop growing. In fact, they can reach up to 3 feet in length. They use their oversized teeth to pull their huge bodies out of the water and break holes in the ice. Sometimes male walruses also use their tusks to win territory or impress females, who also have tusks of their own.

FUN FACT!
Walruses are huge and heavy! Fully grown, they can weigh up to 3,000 pounds.

Why Are Walruses So Chubby?

Walruses have a thick layer of blubber that keeps them warm in the freezing temperatures of their icy homes. Even colder than the land is the water, where walruses lose heat up to 27 times faster. Luckily, their blubber helps them stay warm at temperatures as low as -30°F.

Why do sea lions bark like dogs?

Sea lions bark to show other sea lions how tough they are. For example, a male sea lion might bark to compete for a mate or to scare other males away from his territory. To potential mates, barking means "Come here!" To potential competitors, barking means "Stay away, buddy!" Sea lions are far from dogs, however. The fact that they sound like them is just a coincidence!

STELLER SEA LION

Why do sea lions and seals have flippers?

CRABEATER SEAL

A sea lion or seal without flippers would be like a dog or cat without any legs. And, man, would that make it difficult to get around! Sea lions and seals use their strong flippers to paddle through the water and pull themselves across icy landscapes. When most people think of flippers, they think of the little flaps on the sides of sea lions' and seals' bodies, but their tails are technically flippers, too!

Why do seals have such huge eyes?

Seals' huge eyes are one of many features that make hunting underwater easier. Their big pupils are made to open extremely wide, so they can let in light while they're swimming in dark, murky water. Their round lenses are great at focusing, but only when they're swimming. Underwater, their eyes are better than people's eyes, but on land, we've got seals beat in the vision department.

HARBOR SEAL

Why Do Arctic Foxes Have Such Huge Tails?

For the most part, Arctic foxes use their big, bushy tails to stay warm. When they lie down, they wrap their tails around themselves to ward off the cold weather. It's just like a built-in blanket!

ARCTIC FOX

ARCTIC FOX

FUN FACT!
Like cats' tails, Arctic foxes' big, bushy tails also help them keep their balance.

Why do people say "clever as a fox?"

Foxes are incredibly resourceful animals that are great at solving problems and thinking on their paws. Take the Arctic fox, for example. Although they like to eat lemmings and other small rodents, they'll take whatever they can get when food is hard to come by—which can be pretty often in their snow-filled habitats. They'll eat eggs, birds, hares, berries and even other animals' leftovers! If an Arctic fox thinks finding food might be tough, he'll follow polar bears until they catch a seal. When the bears are done eating, the Arctic fox will get its fill on the scraps.

Media Lab Books
For inquiries, call 646-838-6637

Copyright 2015 Topix Media Lab

Published by Topix Media Lab
14 Wall Street, Suite 4B
New York, NY 10005

ISBN-10:1-942556-02-0
ISBN-13:978-1-942556-02-2

CEO, Co-Founder Tony Romando
COO, Co-Founder Bob Lee
Vice President of Sales and New Markets Tom Mifsud
Vice President of Brand Marketing Joy Bomba

Editor-in-Chief Jeff Ashworth
Creative Director Steven Charny
Photo Director Dave Weiss
Content Editor Bailey Bryant
Senior Editor James Ellis, Johnna Rizzo, Lesley Savage
Art Director Elizabeth Neal
Managing Editor Courtney Kerrigan
Associate Editor Tim Baker
Copy Editor Holland Baker
Photo Editor Meg Reinhardt
Assistant Photo Editor Lindsay Pogash
Senior Designer Kyla Paolucci
Designer Bryn Waryan
Photo Assistant Kelsey Pillischer
Junior Analyst Shiva Sujan
Editorial Assistants Helena Pike, Lauren Sheffield

Answer Key

How many of the questions did you answer correctly? After you've mastered each quiz, use your new knowledge to test your friends!

Page 17: A; Page 23: B; Page 36: B; Page 40: A; Page 49: A; Page 52: C; Page 58: A; Page 65: B; Page 71: A; Page 76: C; Page 98: B; Page 104: C; Page 110: C; Page 117: C; Page 127: B; Page 131: A; Page 135: B; Page 147: B; Page 164: A

Did you find Pepe?

Page 14, Page 22, Page 46, Page 55, Page 68, Page 81, Page 87, Page 101, Page 109, Page 119, Page 130, Page 138, Page 148

All photos of Jack Hanna: Jack Hanna. All other photos Shutterstock except: Suzi Hanna: p23, 83, 121. Rick A. Prebeg/World Class Images: p15, 124. Heather Robertson/iStock/Thinkstock: p13. Jupiterimages/iStock/Thinkstock: p79. chargerv8/iStock/Thinkstock: p151. Steve Greer/iStock: p80. dagut/iStock: p184. Glenn Williams/National Institute of Standards and Technology: p163.

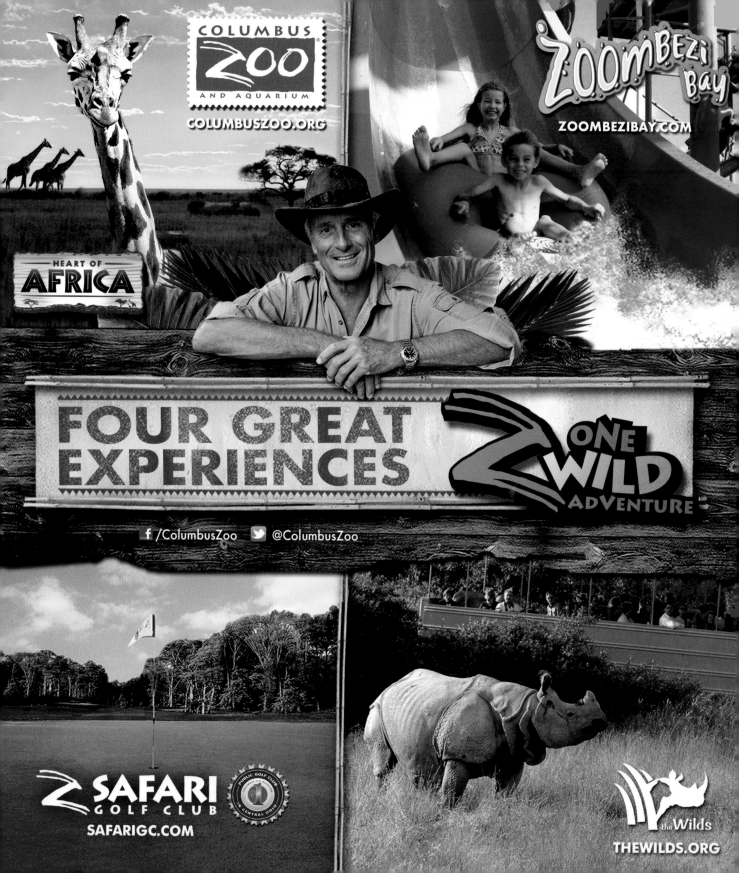

ADOPT AN ANIMAL

POUNCE ON A GREAT OPPORTUNITY!

STARTING AT **$50**, YOUR ADOPTION PACKAGE INCLUDES A PERSONALIZED ADOPTION CERTIFICATE, AND MAKES A UNIQUE GIFT FOR ALL OCCASIONS.

ADOPT YOUR FAVORITE TODAY!

*PLUSH AVAILABILITY SUBJECT TO CHANGE

The End!